EXPLORING HISTORY
The Great War 1914-18

DOROTHY MORRISON

Oliver & Boyd

Contents

Introduction 3
1. Joining the Army 5
2. In the News 10
3. The Western Front 14
4. Life at Home – The Browns and the Schmidts 21
5. Women in Wartime 25
6. Brave Men and Women 29
7. The War of Words 32
8. Looking at the Evidence 36
9. It Stopped at 11 o'clock 38
Index 40
Sources Inside back cover

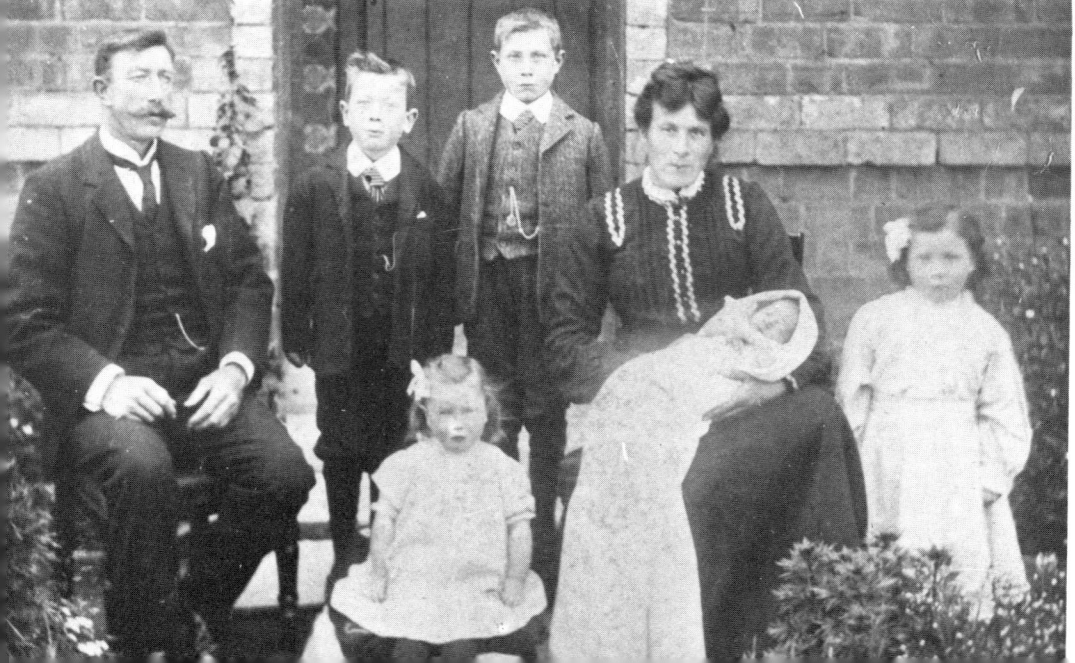

The Brown family

Topics for Workguides

1. Joining the Army
2. In the News
3. The Western Front
4. Life at Home
5. Women in Wartime
6. Brave Men and Women
7. The War of Words
8. Looking at the Evidence
9. It Stopped at 11 o'clock

Acknowledgments

Many of the illustrations in this book are from the author's private collection. Those on pages 5, 6, 13, 16, 17, 19, 20, 25, 26, 27, 28, 29(top), 36, 37, 38 and 39 are reproduced by permission of the Imperial War Museum. The illustration on page 30 is reproduced by permission of the Mansell Collection. The quotation from Siegfried Sassoon's 'Suicide in the Trenches' is reprinted by kind permission of Mr G. T. Sassoon. The cartoons on pages 8, 23, 31 and 34 are from *Punch*.
Maps and plan by Stephen Gibson

Oliver & Boyd
Robert Stevenson House
1-3 Baxter's Place
Leith Walk
Edinburgh EH1 3BB
A Division of Longman Group Ltd.

First published 1981
Fourth impression 1986

This edition © Oliver & Boyd 1981

All rights reserved. No part of this publication may be reproduced, stored in a retrieval system, or transmitted in any form or by any means, electronic, mechanical, photocopying, recording or otherwise, without prior written permission of the Publishers.

ISBN 0 05 003416 2
Produced by Longman Group (FE) Ltd
Printed in Hong Kong

Introduction

The Brown Family

The picture on the left of the Brown family was taken in 1896 soon after their youngest son, Bill, was born. The other boys are ten-year-old John and Joe, aged eight. The girls are Lizzie and Flo.

Mr Brown was a tailor. When he became foreman in a small factory, the family moved to live in Glasgow. In 1905 another child, Annie, was born.

By 1914 most of the family was grown up. Only Annie was still at school.

John was married and had a baby son. He worked as a coalman. The work was hard, especially when he delivered coal to houses up five flights of stairs. However, he earned a good wage, thirty-four shillings* a week.

Joe had a good job as a butcher. Although he earned less than John, he was able to buy meat cheaply.

Lizzie, now nearly twenty-four, had worked in the grocer's shop near her home since she left school at thirteen. She earned fourteen shillings a week. She was saving hard, for she hoped to marry Walter McNab as soon as they had enough money to furnish a house.

Her sister Flo was in service. She worked as a housemaid in a big house in the west end of the city. Her pay was twenty-eight shillings a *month*. On Wednesday afternoons and Sunday evenings she had time off to come home.

The family was proud of Bill. He was training to be a mechanic in an engineering factory. One day he planned to start his own small garage.

1. Make a list of the Brown family. Opposite each name write the job that person had in 1914. Mrs Brown, like most married women, did not go out to work.
2. What was considered a good wage for a man in 1914?
3. How much did Flo earn? What other benefits might she have in her job?

* *You will find a note about shillings and pence on page 4.*

Annie Brown aged twelve

Lizzie worked in a grocer's shop like this

The Brown's House

The Browns lived in a two-room-and-kitchen flat on the third floor of a tenement building. The rent was four shillings a week.

1. *Look at the plan of the Brown's flat. The parents slept in a bed recess in the kitchen. Where did the rest of the family sleep?*

The toilet was on the half-landing below. Two other families shared it. Mrs Brown cooked on a kitchen range heated by a coal fire. The house was lit by gas lamps.

The Family Budget

When her family was young, Mrs Brown found it hard to make ends meet. It was easier once they were working.

Things cost much less than they do now as you can see in this list of 1914 prices.

Coal	1/3d per cwt bag	
Meat	1/- per lb	NOTE
Butter	9d per lb	20/- [twenty
Bread	3d per loaf	shillings] = £1
Margarine	6d per lb	1/- = 5p
Tea (best)	2/- per lb	12d [twelve
Sugar	2d per lb	pence] = 5p
Lady's dress	6/-	1 cwt = 50 kg
Man's suit	£1-10/-	1 lb = 450 g
Shoes	2/11d per pair	

1. *What would the main expenses be for the Brown family?*
2. *How much would it cost to buy these things today?*

Holiday

In July 1914 the Browns had their first family holiday. They all travelled by train to spend four days at Montrose visiting Uncle John. Everyone enjoyed it. Mrs Brown made up her mind that somehow she would save enough for them all to be together again next year at Montrose.

Sadly next year was very different. Britain was at war.

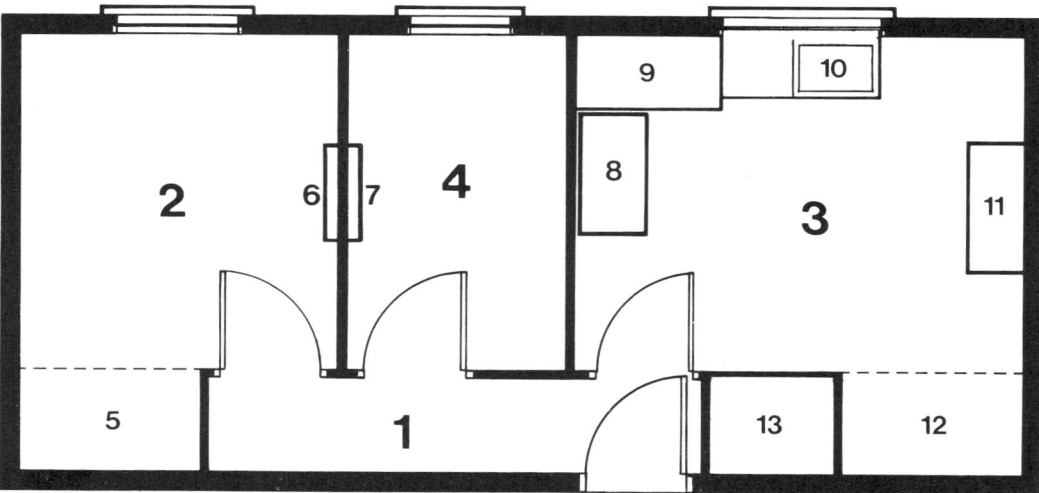

Plan of the Browns' flat

The Brown's' House

1 Lobby
2 Parlour
3 Kitchen
4 Bedroom
5 Bed recess
6/7 Fireplace
8 Dresser
9 Coal bunker
10 Sink
11 Kitchen range
12 Bed recess
13 Press (cupboard)

1. Joining the Army

This poster showing Lord Kitchener became very well known

When the war began in August 1914, Britain sent a small army of 100 000 men to France. The soldiers were well trained and fought well but a much larger army was needed to win the war.

Volunteers

People began to realise the war would not be over quickly. Lord Kitchener, the Minister for War, was a very popular British general and appealed for volunteers to join the army.

Bill Brown came home late one evening in October 1914 looking pleased and excited. 'I've joined up,' he said. 'Four of us went down after work. We had to stand in line for hours, but there was a band playing the whole time.'

All over Britain eager young men were rushing to join the army. By the middle of September half a million men had joined up.

Not all volunteers were young. Study the picture of men with their recruiting sergeant.
1. *Which man do you think is the youngest?*
2. *Which looks the oldest?*
3. *The men are dressed differently. What does this suggest?*

Recruits with sergeant

WANTED
ROYAL MARINES
FOR DURATION OF WAR OR 12 YEARS SERVICE
AGE 17 to 30, AND THE FOLLOWING RATINGS FOR
ROYAL NAVY – STOKERS
COOKS' MATES
ENGINE-ROOM ARTIFICERS FOR WAR PERIOD, ARMOURERS, CARPENTERS, SHIPWRIGHTS and ELECTRICAL ARTIFICERS. ABSOLUTELY CLEAN HEALTHY LIFE with GOOD FOOD. FREE OUTFIT, PENSIONS and SPLENDID PROSPECTS of Advancement to Persevering Candidates. Handbooks obtained at the Post Office.

APPLY TO NEAREST OFFICES at 392 ARGYLE ST., GLASGOW; 13 WATT ST., GREENOCK; 8 JOHNSTON TERRACE, EDINBURGH; 48 MARICHAL ST., ABERDEEN; 1 ACADEMY STREET, AYR; and 74 HIGH STREET, KIRKCALDY.

3rd LOWLAND (RESERVE) BRIGADE
ROYAL FIELD ARTILLERY
Major D. T. EASTON, T.D., R.F.A. (T.), Commanding.

RECRUITS can now be enlisted, as authority has been received to recruit other 25 per cent of Establishment.
SHOEING SMITHS, SADDLERS, TELEPHONE MECHANICS, GUNNERS, and DRIVERS are wanted. Age 18 to 35 years. All must undertake the Imperial Service obligation.
RIDING SCHOOL DAILY

Apply at HEADQUARTERS
8 NEWTON TERRACE, Charing Cross,
GLASGOW.
D. C. MILLER, Captain, R.F.A.(T.),
Acting Adjutant, 3rd Lowland (Reserve)
Brigade R.F.A.

LOVAT SCOUTS
YEOMANRY

RECRUITS WANTED
MUST BE GOOD RIDERS.

Apply STEWART'S, 569 Argyle Street, Anderston Cross, Glasgow, 1 up, between 5 p.m. and 8 p.m.

8th (RESERVE) BATTALION
THE CAMERONIANS
(SCOTTISH RIFLES)
Lieut-Col ALAN D. KED, T.D., Commanding.

RECRUITS WANTED
To ENROL IN IMPERIAL SERVICE for the
PERIOD of the WAR
HEIGHT, 5 FEET 3 INCHES* and OVER
AGE 19 to 36 YEARS

APPLY AT
HEADQUARTERS,
140 CATHEDRAL STREET, GLASGOW.
Between 9 a.m. and 9 p.m.

Every newspaper carried details of how to join up
(*5 feet 3 inches is about 1.65 metres)

Look at the advertisements for war service on this page.
1. What jobs were available?
2. To accept 'Imperial Service' meant agreeing to go overseas. Why would this be required?
3. In earlier wars cavalry had played an important part. What shows that the cavalry was still considered important in 1914?
4. In 1914 why would the army need a great number of horses?

Getting Men to Join Up

Joe was upset when he heard about Bill. He felt it was unwise to give up a good job. Like many other men he was not keen to fight. Sometimes it was hard to refuse. As he walked along the street he saw posters like the ones on page 6 stuck up on the walls.

1. What were these posters designed to do?
2. If you were a young man then, how would you feel reading them?

Joe's married brother John, the coalman, was interested in joining the army. The pay seemed good and his wife and small son would be provided for.

Look at the advertisement on the right and then answer the questions.
1. What were the three qualifications for joining up?
2. How long would John need to serve in the army?
3. How much would he be paid?
4. What other benefits were there?
5. How much would John's wife and family receive?
6. What pensions might be paid?
7. Where could John be told how to join up?
8. Which posters might have influenced John?
9. Would John's attitude influence Joe? How?

MORE MEN ARE WANTED FOR HIS MAJESTY'S ARMY

WHO MAY ENLIST.
All men who are 5ft. 3ins. and over, medically fit, and between 19 and 38, and all old soldiers up to 45.

TERMS OF ENLISTMENT.
You may join for the period of the War only if you do not want to serve for the ordinary period of the regular soldier. Then, as soon as the War is over, you will be able to return to your ordinary employment.

PAY.
Ordinary Army Pay (the lowest rate of pay is 7s. a week, less 1½d. for Insurance). Food, Clothing, Lodging and Medical Attendance provided free.

SEPARATION ALLOWANCES.
During the War the State, by the payment of Separation Allowance, helps the soldier to maintain his wife, children or dependants. The following are the weekly rates for the wife and children of a private soldier, including the allotment usually required from his pay:—

	Government Separation Allowance s. d.	Largest Allotment required from Soldier. s. d.	Weekly Income Secured to Family. s. d.
For Wife only	9 0	3 6	12 6
" and 1 Child	14 6	3 6	17 6
" and 2 Children	17 6	3 6	21 0

For each additional child an additional Separation Allowance of 2s. is issuable. Families living at the time of enlistment in the London Postal area are allowed by the State 3s. 6d. a week extra as long as they continue to live there.
Fuller particulars as to Separation Allowance, and as to Allowances to the Dependants of Unmarried Soldiers, and to the Motherless Children of Soldiers, can be obtained at any Recruiting Office or Post Office.

PENSIONS for the DISABLED.
Men disabled on service will be entitled after discharge to benefits under the Insurance Act IN ADDITION TO the Pension given by the War Office for partial or total disablement.

PROVISION for WIDOWS and CHILDREN.
The widows and children of soldiers who die on active service will continue to receive their Separation Allowances for a period which will not in any case exceed 26 weeks, and afterwards they will receive, SUBJECT TO CERTAIN QUALIFICATIONS, pensions at various rates.

HOW TO ENLIST.
Go to the nearest Post Office or Labour Exchange. There you will get the address of the nearest Recruiting Office, where you can enlist.

MEN ARE WANTED – ENLIST NOW.

PUBLISHED BY THE PARLIAMENTARY RECRUITING COMMITTEE, 12, DOWNING STREET, S.W. Poster No. 53.

One evening Joe went to the music hall with his girlfriend, Annie. A lady dressed as Britannia sang a song, 'We don't want to lose you, but we think you ought to go!'

Annie told Joe she would like to walk out with a soldier in uniform. Some of her friends were giving out white feathers to men who stayed at home.

One day Joe's employer showed him the notice on the right. He promised that if Joe joined the army he would give him two shillings a week and his job back at the end of the war.

1. Why do you think Annie's friends gave white feathers to men who stayed at home?
2. Who could take on Joe's job in the shop?
3. Would it be easy for Joe to refuse to go? Why?

> 1. HAVE you any fit men between 19 and 38 years of age serving behind your counter who at this moment ought to be serving their country?
> 2. Will you call your male employees together and explain to them that in order to end the War quickly we must have more men?
> 3. Will you tell them what you are prepared to do for them whilst they are fighting for the Empire?
> 4. Have you realised that we cannot have "business as usual" whilst the War continues?
>
> **THE ARMY WANTS MORE MEN TO-DAY**
>
> 5. Could not Women or older men fill their places till the War is over?
>
> **YOUR COUNTRY WILL APPRECIATE THE HELP YOU GIVE.**
>
> ## God Save the King.

Cartoons and jokes about joining up were published in magazines like *Punch*

"How is it you're not at the Front, young man?"
"'Cause there ain't no milk at that end, mum."

So many joined up that in some places there were not enough skilled men left at home to carry on the working of the factories, mines and farms. Older men and many girls and women had to take on these jobs.

1. What types of workers might stay at home?
2. Why would it be unwise for all fit men in Britain to join up?
3. Suggest reasons, *apart from work*, why men might not serve in the army.

MILITARY SERVICE ACT 1916

EVERY UNMARRIED MAN of MILITARY AGE

Not excepted or exempted under this Act

CAN CHOOSE ONE OF TWO COURSES:

(1) He can **ENLIST AT ONCE** and join the Colours without delay;

(2) He can **ATTEST AT ONCE UNDER THE GROUP SYSTEM** and be called up in due course with his Group.

If he does neither, a third course awaits him:

HE WILL BE DEEMED TO HAVE ENLISTED under the Military Service Act **ON THURSDAY, MARCH 2nd, 1916.**

HE WILL BE PLACED IN THE RESERVE, AND BE CALLED UP IN HIS CLASS, as the Military Authorities may determine.

Published by THE PARLIAMENTARY RECRUITING COMMITTEE, LONDON. POSTER No 156.   Printed by DAVID ALLEN & SONS, Ld. Harrow, Mdx.

Conscription

As the war went on, more and more troops were killed or seriously wounded. The government brought in the Military Service Act in 1916. This introduced *conscription* which meant that all unmarried men of the right age could be made to join the army whether they liked it or not.

1. *What three things might happen?*
2. *Why would men be wise to join before 2nd March?*

On the right you can see the picture Bill sent home of himself in uniform. His mother gave it a place of honour on the mantelpiece. Then John and Joe joined up as well.

1. *If you were Mrs Brown, how might you feel?*
2. *If you were Mr Brown, how might you feel?*

2. In the News

On 1st August 1914 the message below came over the tape machine to newspapers in Britain. No one was really surprised. During the summer months the countries of Europe had grown closer and closer to war. Britain tried hard to keep the peace but by 4th August, Britain also had joined the War.

1. Which two countries are mentioned in the message?
2. Which words in the message are shortened to 'T' and 'O'?
3. How was the German declaration of war announced?

Mr Brown read the newspaper carefully every night after work. Sometimes he found it very hard to understand just what was happening. Each country seemed to be affected by what happened elsewhere.

If Russia comes in, Germany will certainly back Austria, and France will be dragged in, not to speak of Italy and minor nations. And what of Britain? Can we keep out? We could not let France go under, at any price. No; we must be all one now – one for peace if it may be, and one for war if it must be.

The Times, 2nd August, 1914

1. Which countries are mentioned in the newspaper article?
2. What large modern nations are not mentioned?

Airships

Until the war began, most people in Britain had not seen even a picture of an airship. No one realised how people at home might be threatened by an attack from the air.

In 1915 the government issued the poster on page 11.

1. What were people told to do if they saw an enemy aircraft?
2. What two things were they told not to do?
3. (a) What information should be given if the enemy aircraft was seen in a country district? (b) How would this be useful?
4. Would it be easy to tell the difference between British and German aircraft? Give reasons.

```
10-25PM. REUTERS TEL. GERMANY DECLARS
WAR ON RUSSIA. ST PETERSBURG. AUG. 1
T GERMAN AMBASSADOR IN T NAME O HIS
GOVT HANDED TO T FOREIGN MINISTRY A
DECLARATION O WAR AT 7-30 THIS
EVENING. REUTER. 10-27
```

The Browns were shocked to read this story.

On the evening of Wednesday, October 13, another aerial attack was directed against London.

The enemy's vessels flew high, no doubt in order to prevent as far as possible the danger of damage or destruction from anti-aircraft guns. The darkening of the city together with the height at which the aircraft travelled certainly prevented the enemy from discovering the exact position of places of importance.

Daily Record, October, 1915

1. Which city was attacked?
2. Why did the Zeppelins fly high?
3. Why did the Germans find it hard to spot important places?

The danger from Zeppelin raids was cut down by using night-flying fighter planes of the Royal Naval Air Service.

Good News!

Sometimes the news Mr Brown read in his evening paper was good. He enjoyed reading this story out to his wife as she cooked the tea.

Pte. George Ferguson, 9th Gordon Highlanders, was officially reported killed on September 25. His death was lamented by all his friends, for he was a popular young man – he played with Carluke Milton Rovers Football Club.
One day this week his friends in Hill Road, Motherwell, received a letter from the 'killed' man himself stating that he is well but a prisoner in Germany.

His friends are willing to accept the evidence of the soldier's own handwriting that he is still to the fore, notwithstanding the official declaration that he is not. Several similar cases have occurred in Motherwell.

Daily Record, November 1916

1. Tell this newspaper story in your own words.
2. Explain why such a mistake might happen.

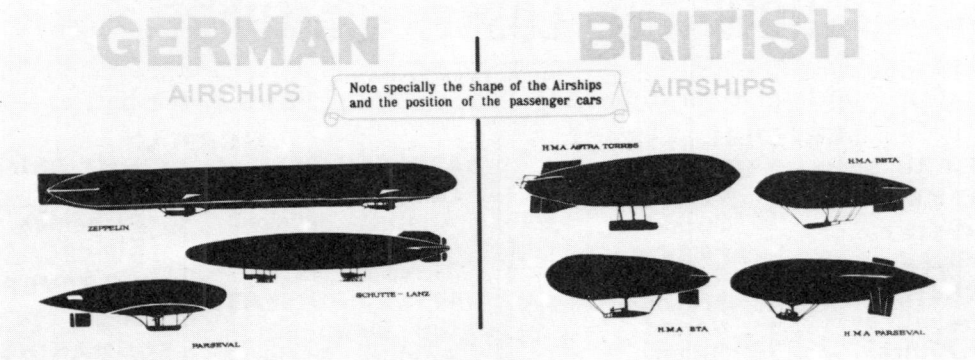

The War at Sea

Mr Brown's hands shook as he looked at the headlines one Sunday morning. Like most people, he was sure that the British navy was the biggest and best in the world. It could not be beaten. He could not understand why so many British ships had been lost.

Both Britain and Germany had big fleets of warships but the fleets met only once, at the Battle of Jutland. The Germans had planned to trap a small part of the British fleet. The British had found out about this plan. They sent a large fleet to take the Germans by surprise. The German naval weapons were better. To save the fleet, the British commander sacrificed some ships. In the end the German fleet broke off fighting and ran for port.

1. When was this big battle fought?
2. In which area did fighting take place?
3. Which country appears to have lost more ships?
4. Both the British and the Germans claimed Jutland as a great victory. Why do you think they did this?

THE SEA OF DEATH
COPENHAGEN, Saturday.
Fishing cutters arriving to-day at ports on the west coast of Jutland report that all along the course followed by the great naval battle the North Sea is strewn with the bodies of British and German naval officers and men and with wreckage of all kinds.

The captain of the Swedish steamer Tana, which has arrived from Leith, reports that on Thursday morning he sighted in the North Sea a wreck, which proved to be the stern of a cruiser.

Around the wreck were about fifty bodies of Englishmen and Germans, while three still living German petty officers were aboard it and were rescued. They were the survivors of the German torpedo boat V 48. – Central News.

Sunday Pictorial, 4 June 1916

In 1917 the news was gloomy. Although the newspapers gave no details, it was clear that German submarines were causing great damage to ships coming to and leaving Britain. Food and war materials were very short.

'The Yanks are Coming!'

The headline news on 2nd April, 1917 cheered everyone in Britain. The USA joined the war on the side of the Allies.

1. Why was it such good news that the United States was fighting on the same side as Britain?
2. What help would the Americans be able to send to the Allies?
3. How would the Germans feel about this?

News from Russia

The Browns did not know much about Russia but they grew more and more worried as they read the news from Russia in 1917.

Russian soldiers had fought bravely, but they were very short of weapons and food. They had begun to lose faith in their ruler, the Czar, and the army leaders. Russians at home were suffering badly from the war. They were very short of food and tired of fighting. At last people turned against the government, and revolution broke out. The Czar was overthrown. Another leader, Lenin, promised he would end the war and help the people. After some months he became ruler of Russia and made peace with Germany.

1. On which side had Russia been fighting?
2. What happened to the Czar?
3. What promise did Lenin make?
4. Would the Allies want Lenin to rule Russia? Say why.
5. How would it help Germany if Russia made peace?

Let us now look more closely at how the war began.

American troops welcomed by the crowds as they march through London with the Stars and Stripes flying

3. The Western Front

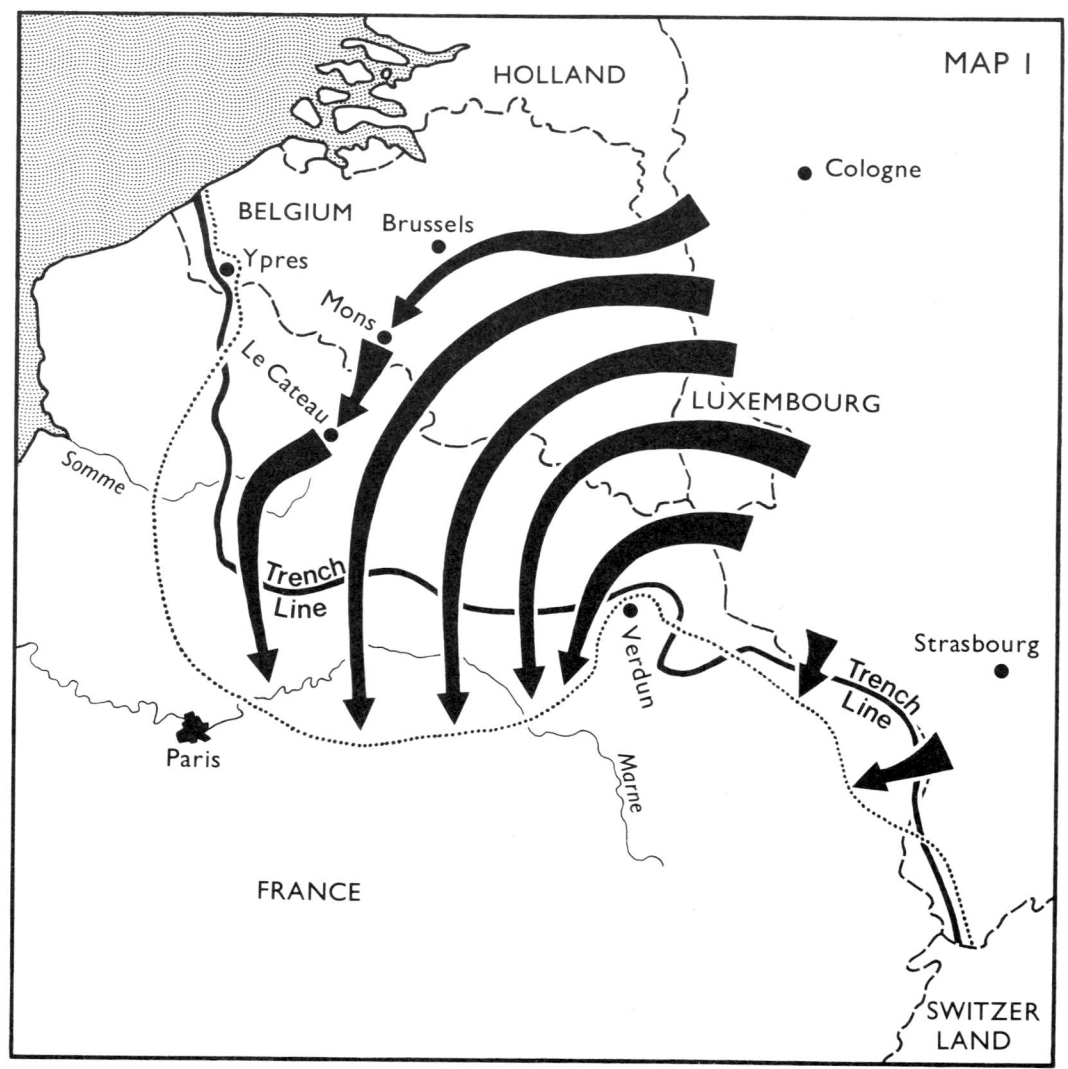

When the war started, the strong German army quickly moved through Belgium to attack France. The small British force held them back for a time at *Mons* but had to fall back to just north of Paris. The French soldiers were ready waiting at the River Marne.

The arrows on the map show the seven points of the German advance. The dotted line shows how far they had reached by the first week of September 1914.

After the Battle of the *Marne*, the Germans were forced to retreat. They turned north to get round the line of the French and British troops. But they were held back at *Ypres* where over 50 000 British troops were killed.

Neither side could move forward. Both armies dug lines of trenches stretching from the coast of Belgium to Switzerland. This was the *Western Front*.

By the end of 1914 there were three main areas of fighting which are shown on Map 2.

1. From Map 2, list the countries shown in capital letters which were allies of Britain.
2. List the countries underlined which sided with Germany. Why do you think these were called the Central Powers?
3. Which of the Allies would fight mainly on the Western Front?
4. Which of the Allies would fight mainly against the Central Powers on the Eastern Front?
5. Which other countries later joined the Allies?
6. Which one later joined the Central Powers?

On the Western Front the lines of trenches hardly moved for four years. Millions of men died and millions more were wounded as each side tried to break through. For example, in the German attack on the French fortress of *Verdun* in 1916, the French lost 315 000 men and the Germans 282 323 but no one really won in the end.

When the British launched a major attack on the *Somme* in 1916, the Germans lost almost half a million men, while the Allies lost 623 000 but only moved forward a very short distance.

War in the Trenches

Bill Brown was sent to the Western Front three months after he joined up. His short training had not prepared him for the horror of war in the trenches. He spent New Year's Day 1915 up to his ankles in mud.

This eye-witness account of life in the trenches appeared in a newspaper.

During the last three days the weather although milder has continued very wet, aggravating the hardships of the men in the trenches. The wet clay is so adhesive that even the stoutest of boots will sometimes give way under the strain. In order to keep as dry as possible many of the men go barefoot down the long communication trenches, and only put on their boots and socks when in the better drained fire trenches. Even when active operations are not in progress life in the fighting line is not so dull as might be supposed, for not only is continual work required to keep the trenches dry and to

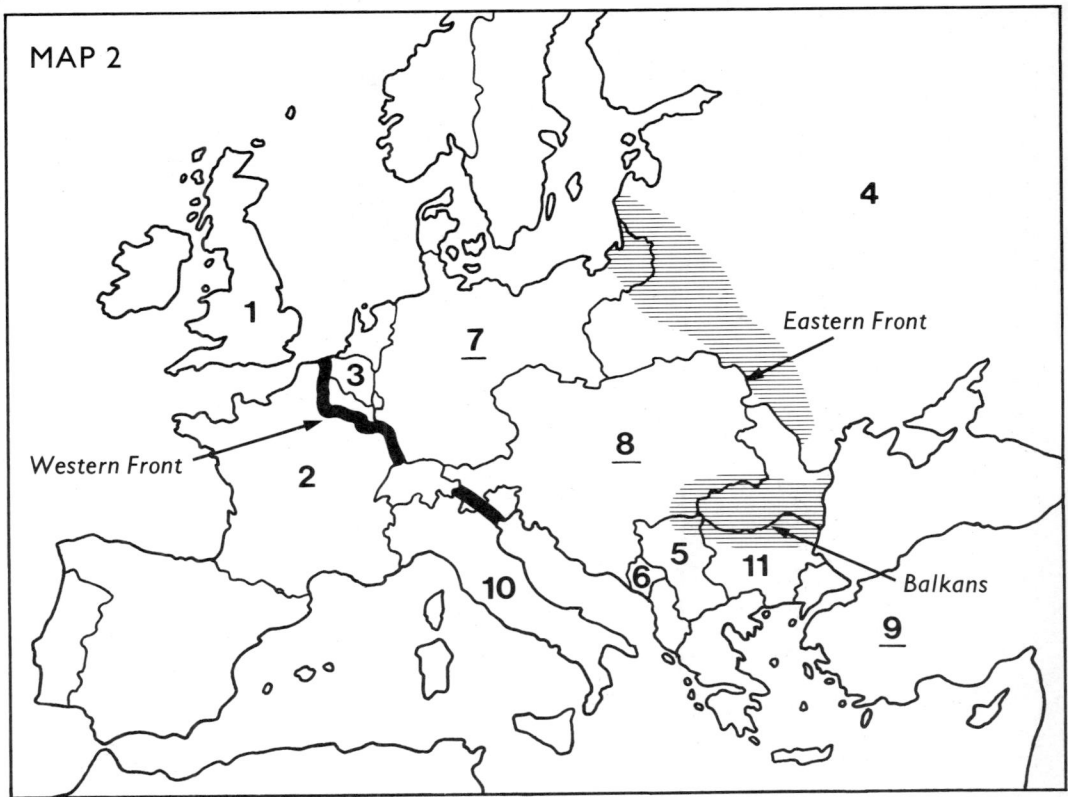

1. BRITAIN
2. FRANCE
3. BELGIUM
4. RUSSIA
5. SERBIA
6. MONTENEGRO
7. Germany
8. Austria-Hungary
9. Turkey
10. Italy
11. Bulgaria

(Bulgaria later joined the Central Powers and Italy and USA joined the Allies.)

(above) These men are carrying containers of hot food to soldiers at the front line.
(below) Water was another important thing that had to be carried up to the front line trenches. (Dixies were the containers usually used for stew or tea.)

prevent the earth in places from falling in, but there is the continual effort on each side to gain the mastery in sniping, in sapping, and in the bombardment by trench mortars and hand grenades, there is the construction and repair of barbed wire entanglements, and the digging of trenches by night within close range of the enemy's sentries, and the carrying of messages by day over open ground swept by fire.

Daily Record and Mail, 6 January 1915

1. How did wet weather make life worse for the men in the trenches?
2. Were only the Allies affected by the weather?
3. Why did the men go barefoot in the communication trenches?
4. Why would trenches be dug at night rather than in the daytime?
5. A sap was a trench built underground towards the enemy position. What is meant by sapping?
6. What made carrying messages difficult in the daytime?
7. Trenches in the front line were divided into bays with only five or six men in each bay. Suggest a reason for this.
8. Often there was no hot food. What else might the soldiers have to eat?
9. Why would water be carefully used at the front line?
10. What other important supplies do you think would be carried along the communication trenches?

Not every soldier served in the front line.

There were 20 000 men in a division, but only 2000 of them would be in the front line at any one time. The usual arrangement over a month was to spend about four days in the front line, four days in the support trenches (where the kitchens and stores were) behind the front line, eight days in reserve and the other days resting. During the Battle of the Somme, Bill Brown's section was unlucky enough to be left 29 days in the front line without being relieved.

1. Why do you think men were usually left in the front line for only four or five days at a time?
2. How do you think Bill would feel after such a long spell of duty?

In a Dug-Out

War was not what Bill had imagined. He hardly ever saw the enemy. In the front line he was advised to keep his head down in case a German sniper shot him. He spent most of the time, when he was not actually fighting, in a hole in the ground called a dug-out, like the men in the picture on the right.

1. What are the men in the dug-out doing?
2. Does it look comfortable? What would happen when it rained heavily?

Keeping Healthy

Soldiers were issued with a small booklet telling them how to keep healthy. Here is part of what it said about keeping clean.

A dug-out. There is a poem about a dug-out in Workguide 3

Most men wash their faces and even their hands, but parts covered by clothes are often forgotten. The following should be washed every day, when possible:

1. Between the legs and buttocks.
2. The feet and toes.
3. The armpits.

Clothing   Socks get quickly dirty and the custom of some men is to continue to wear one pair for a week. By this want of arrangement, it is impossible to preserve hard, clean feet.

Army Health Manual

1. Why would it be difficult for men in the trenches to follow this advice? Give several reasons.

THE SUPER LEATHER FOR SOLES

Keeps Tommy's feet dry – all the time – in the trenches or on the march. Even the mud of Flanders cannot penetrate Dri-ped.

What Bill Brown hated most were the lice and rats in the trenches. Rats were everywhere for there were plenty of dead bodies for them to feed on. Soldiers joked about them but they really hated them.

Rats

I want to write a poem, yet I find I have no theme,
'Rats' are no subject for an elegy,
Yet they fill my waking moments, and when star-shells softly gleam,
'Tis the rats who spend the midnight hours with me.

On my table in the evening they will form 'Battalion mass' [*a marching order*],
They will open tins of bully [*corned beef*] with their teeth,
And should a cake be sent by some friend at home, alas!
They will extricate it from its cardboard sheath [*packing*].

B.E.F. Times

1. Why do you think the soldiers hated rats so much?
2. Why do you think they joked about them?

Gas Attacks

A new weapon used in the First World War was gas. On the Western Front in April 1915 the Germans released gas from cylinders and took French troops completely by surprise.

GERMAN POISON GAS
Effective French Masks

A TRAGIC STORY
(By Private Wire)

London, Thursday. – I informed you the other day that, according to a French officer back from the front, our anti-gas masks are now perfectly efficient, says the Paris correspondent of the "Daily Telegraph."

This was not always the case.

The masks first given out to the French troops were effectual against gas, but a serious drawback was that the wearer could not speak through his mask.

Here is a tragic and also a heroic story of the consequence –

A French regiment was in the trenches, and the enemy having a favourable wind sent a wave of gas. Men and officers put on masks, except the colonel, who if he had done so could not have given orders. The colonel soon fell, suffocated, and the next officer in seniority instantly took off his mask and commanded. He also fell. Two more officers did the same and fell. The men then charged, exasperated by the loss of four officers, and repelled the attack.

Apart from asphyxiating gas, one of the Germans' ingenious inventions, the enemy had also manufactured some poisonous shells producing blood poisoning when a wound was inflicted, but it seems that the French having threatened reprisals the enemy, who used some of these blood poisoning shells at the beginning of the war, has given them up.

Evening Times, 27 April 1915

When Mr Brown read about gas attacks he thought it wicked, but both sides used gas all during the war. Some gas affected the lungs and throat, but mustard gas burned the skin.

1. How was gas carried across to the enemy?
2. What were the drawbacks of early gas masks?
3. Why would gas be used?
4. What danger might gas have for the troops using it?
5. Do you think these French troops had been in a gas attack before? Say why.

The Sounds of Battle

Bill never grew used to the many different noises at the front. The guns hardly stopped firing day or night. Between July and November 1916, in the Battle of the Somme, 900 heavy and 1100 light guns lay along a front 16 kilometres long. Two million shells were fired and the noise was so great that Londoners nearly 500 kilometres away could hear the sound of gunfire.

If a high explosive shell with a thick steel casing fell in a dug-out, any soldiers not killed at once might be buried alive. Shrapnel shells, which had a thin casing filled with lead pellets, would burst in the air and spray splinters above the open trenches. Almost three-quarters of the wounds inflicted by the end of the war were shell wounds. Machine guns could fire many bullets quickly and were greatly feared by foot soldiers.

After the Battle of the Somme, one soldier wrote in his diary

> A damnable sight. About the worst I have ever known. Not for a single moment has the shelling stopped. Everyone is badly shaken.
>
> H. Allen

Another one wrote

> After a thunderous crash in our ears, a young boy began to cry for his mother in a thin, boyish voice. 'Mam, Mam....' He had not been hit but was frightened and crying quietly.
>
> H. Griffith

1. What might the continuous noise of firing do to men in the trenches?
2. What different types of shells might be used?
3. Some soldiers in the trenches suffered from shell-shock. What do you think this means?
4. What would be the problems of wearing body armour like that in the photograph?

Sometimes, because they had been under heavy fire for such a long time, soldiers became so afraid they refused to fight. They might be shot for cowardice.

Soldier in anti-splinter armour

DEATH SENTENCES AT THE FRONT

The Under-Secretary for War was asked if it is the practice of the War Office, in cases where private soldiers have been court martialled and put to death at the front for disobeying orders, etc. to notify their parents that such sentence had been carried out by means of open postcard, and if so, will steps be taken to alter such methods?

Mr Tennant replied, 'Record officers are provided with forms on which to notify deaths. It has been decided that, as in these cases their relatives were bound to know sooner or later the circumstances of the death, it was better that they should be informed at once.'

Daily Record and Mail, September 1915

1. Why do you think such soldiers were put to death?
2. Do you think it was right to do this? Say why.
3. How would the parents of such soldiers feel when they heard that their sons had been put to death?

Some soldiers made sketches and drawings. The sketch below of a trench was made by an Edinburgh soldier.

1. *Explain the notice on the left of the picture.*
2. *The long box shape behind the officer's head is a periscope. Why might this be useful, do you think?*

The photograph on the right shows a German sniper's post high up in a tree. From here he could see a good distance and pick his target carefully. This was how Bill Brown died in March 1917, when a sniper's bullet hit him in the head. He had completed two years and three months of service on the Western Front.

4. Life at Home – The Browns and the Schmidts

NOTHING is to be written on this side except the date and signature of the sender. Sentences not required may be erased. If anything else is added the post card will be destroyed.

I am quite well.

I have been admitted into hospital

{ sick } and am going on well.
{ wounded } and hope to be discharged soon.

I am being sent down to the base.

I have received your { letter dated _____
                       telegram „ _____
                       parcel „ _____ }

Letter follows at first opportunity.

I have received no letter from you
{ lately.
{ for a long time.

Signature only. } Wallace

Date ~~bbb~~ 8/1/17

[Postage must be prepaid on any letter or post card addressed to the sender of this card.]

(*3871) Wt. W3497-293 4,500m. 7/16 J.J.K. & Co., Ltd.

When John joined the Army, his wife, Margaret, and the baby moved in with the Browns. Mrs Brown looked after the baby, and Margaret took a job in the factory where Mr Brown worked. Now it made army uniforms instead of men's suits.

Mrs Brown was very anxious about Bill for the only news she had of him was a Field Service postcard like the one on the left.

1. Write out the full message on the Field Service post card.
2. The sender was in the front line.
   (a) Why did he not write a letter?
   (b) What would happen if he wrote anything else on the card?

War Comforts

In every town there was a war fund to send 'comforts' [useful gifts] to the troops.

At school Annie helped to knit scarves, socks and balaclava helmets. Mrs Brown sent parcels herself to her three boys. For Joe's birthday she sent him a packet of cigarettes and a fountain pen. Every Saturday she went to help in the canteen for soldiers at the railway station.

1. Give three reasons why Mrs Brown chose a 'Swan' pen.
2. Why was the station a good place for a soldier's canteen?

ON SOLDIER'S INK

SWAN

BECAUSE it is not a 'self-filling' pen.

Because it can be filled with SWAN Ink Tablets – the only form of ink available to the soldier in the field.

Because the Postmaster-General prohibits the sending of glass bottles, and bottled ink cannot therefore be procured in the trenches.

Because the SWAN has no works to get out of order – always ready, ever dependable.

Because by sending a SWAN you will avoid disappointment.

Why the SWAN is the best Fountain Pen for the Front

Newspaper advertisement

On Leave

Lizzie's boyfriend, Walter, came home on leave from the Navy. The week passed quickly. Every night Lizzie and Walter went to the moving pictures, a music hall or a tea dance. 'I might never see him again,' Lizzie explained. 'We'll enjoy ourselves while we can.'

Now cheer up, I'll be back soon. -

Lizzie was right. Walter sent this postcard but sadly he was killed at the Battle of Jutland.

Casualties

In every newspaper there were long lists each day of young men killed or wounded. Few families escaped. There were so many widows, and parents who had lost their sons, that people stopped wearing complete black mourning clothes as they had in the past.

SCOTS CASUALTIES
Today's Official Lists

London. Saturday – The following casualties amongst warrant officers, non-commissioned officers and men are reported under various dates.

The town shown against each soldier's name is the home of his next-of-kin, except when followed by the abbreviation 'enlt.', when it is his place of enlistment.

KILLED
Royal Scots – Fraser (2366), J. (Portobello).
The Black Watch – Thomas (2347), W. H. (Leslie).
Highland Light Infantry – Brown (2732), A. G. (Glasgow); Ingram (29216), C. (Glasgow); Torrance (29190), Corporal W. (Glasgow).
Argyll & Sutherland Highlanders – Cameron (8374), Sergeant C. (Greenock); Flynn (8298), Lance-Corporal W. (Paisley); Shields (7845), Lance-Corporal D. (Grangemouth).

DIED OF WOUNDS
Cameronians (Scottish Rifles) – Boslem (3497), D. (Tarbrax); Paterson (8142), S. (Paisley); Wilson (12755), J. (Dundee).
Gordon Highlanders – Adams (4832), A. H. (Aberdeen); Fraser (4301), A. (Aberdeen); Roy (11912), A. (Fochabers); Ross (1339), Sergeant W. (Glenkindie); Thomson (11842), W. (Keith).

WOUNDED
Highland Light Infantry – M'Innes (4616), Sergeant D. (Glasgow); M'Neillie (5778), H. (Glasgow).
Seaforth Highlanders – Brenner (580), W. (Aberdeen); Morrison (3507), C. (Greenock); Mossman (5328), A. (Ibrox); Ritchie (1135), G. (Hopeman); Wyllie (3201), J. (Elgin).

MISSING
King's Own Scottish Borderers – Descaps (23287), B. (Lockerbie); Munro (16311), Acting Corporal B. (Methil); Murray (6390), R. (Dumfries); Pettitt (200000), P. (Castleford); Purvis (18428), J. (Coldstream); Sanderson (23262), W. (Killearn).

Daily Record and Mail, September 1915

Food Shortages

Other things made life difficult for those at home. Britain did not grow enough food to feed the people. Nearly 80% of the wheat and 40% of the meat Britain needed came from abroad. When German submarines sank ships coming to Britain, there were bad shortages. Margarine, fats, milk, bacon and tea were very scarce. Sugar and butter almost disappeared. People had to wait in long queues for food.

In 1917 the government asked people to limit themselves to small amounts of bread, meat and sugar and eventually meat was rationed [each person was allowed the same amount]. The price of bread went up greatly.

1. Which foods were difficult to get?
2. Why would shopping take longer?
3. Why would the price of bread and other foods go up?
4. How might some people take advantage of food shortages?
5. Would people eat as well as they had before the war? Say why.

Strikes

One result of wartime difficulties in 1917 was a fortnight of serious strikes. The Prime Minister appealed to everyone to keep working.

1. Why was it important that munitions factories kept working day and night?

TRADE UNIONS AND WAR MUNITIONS

Addressing the Trades Union Congress yesterday, Mr. Lloyd George said, 'The Government cannot win without you.' This is a war of material. In order to work the 16 new arsenals and the 11 under construction we want 80,000 more skilled men and 200,000 more unskilled men. The country is not doing its best. Only 15 per cent of the available machinery is working night shift in turning out cannons and rifles and war material.

The Government intends to turn over to unskilled people the work they can do, reserving highly skilled work that can only be done by those of great skill and training.

Daily Record, November 1915

SELF OR COUNTRY?

COVENTRY STRIKER. "IF I WAS A SOLDIER AND THEY TRIED TO SHIFT ME TO ANOTHER PART OF THE LINE JUST AS I WAS COMFORTABLE I'D DOWN TOOLS."
FIGHTING MAN. "NO, YOU WOULDN'T, IF YOU WERE A SOLDIER YOU'D BE OUT TO DOWN HUNS."

The Schmidts – A German Family

Life for German families was even harder. The Schmidt family in Berlin had joined the cheering crowds when Germany went to war in 1914. They were confident, in the first three years of the war, that Germany would win. The older son, Hans, was fighting in France and sent letters when he could.

British ships were able to stop Germany getting goods by sea. This caused shortages. There was no coffee but you could buy a good substitute made from a mixture of roasted barley, rye, chicory and figs. After the bad harvest of 1916 all food was scarce. It was impossible to get soap. Frau Schmidt queued for hours for bread, fat, meat or butter which were all rationed.

1. Why were there food shortages in Germany?
2. What goods were very scarce?
3. Mention two things Mrs Brown and Frau Schmidt might have in common.

At school Franz and Elsa Schmidt were told to collect acorns, chestnuts and nettles to help the war effort. There was a great shortage of metal and all spare goods made of copper were collected by children from houses round about. Their teacher explained to Franz and Elsa how old bones could be useful to make glue for aeroplanes, glycerine for explosives and fertilisers for farming. Even hair could be used to make machine belting.

1. How might Franz and Elsa try to help Germany win the war?

1918 was a bad year for Germany. The shortages and difficulties caused strikes. Hans was killed. Herr Schmidt, working long hours on poor food, became ill. For the first time Franz and Elsa realised Germany might lose the war. It was hard to believe that the country they loved could be defeated.

German children help the war effort

5. Women in Wartime

Flo Brown had never really enjoyed working as a housemaid. Sometimes she wished she worked in a shop like her sister or as a dressmaker like her friend, Mary.

Women's War Work

Her whole life was changed when she saw this poster one Wednesday on her afternoon off.

Instead of going home she went to the Labour Exchange to enrol.

1. Flo felt she was helping to win the war. Give another reason why she might want to change her job.
2. Flo was given a job making shells. Why was this job not kept mostly for men?
3. Why do you think over 400 000 women left domestic service during the war?

WOMEN SHELLMAKERS

SKILFUL AND EFFICIENT WORKERS

Much has been said and written regarding the work of the patriotic women who have undertaken men's work on the tramways and railways and in factories and shops in order to release men to serve with the colours, but so far very little has been made known regarding the great success of those women working in munitions factories.

The women and girls employed have shown an extraordinary aptitude for the work, and this, coupled with their great enthusiasm, has enabled them not only to develop speedily into efficient and skilled workers, but has enabled them to maintain a wonderfully high standard of output.

Evening Times, February 1916

1. Look at the first paragraph of the newspaper article. What other work had women taken over from men?
2. Was the employment of women shellworkers a success? Say why.

Mrs Margaret Morrison, born in 1893, remembers her work in Beardmores, the largest manufacturers of shells in the west of Scotland:

Until then I had worked as a laundry maid on a big estate. Most of us had never worked on machines before. We were given a week's instruction, by one of the foremen. After a while they said we could do as well as any of the skilled workmen. Of course we didn't get the same pay. Some of the very heavy jobs such as setting up machines were done by men but we girls could do nearly all the work ourselves. I worked a drilling machine. Later I was a pattern maker. Working in the explosives section could be dangerous but there were no serious accidents in our factory. We worked a twelve-hour shift but the pay was good. On the night shift we got extra pay. One week when I worked full seven days, I earned nearly £3. My father never got that much in his life.

1. (a) What was Mrs Morrison's job before she became a shellmaker?
   (b) How much training was she given?
   (c) Do you think she liked the work? Say why.
2. Why do you think women shellworkers were well paid?
3. Why were they paid less than men?

Women do Men's Work

Lizzie took a very different job. She became one of Glasgow's first lady tramcar drivers at a wage of 18/6d per week.

All over Britain women took all sorts of jobs which released men to fight. Some of the jobs needed strength as well as skill, such as delivering coal, blacksmith's work and sweeping chimneys.

Sometimes men resented women taking over jobs. They thought their wages might go down if women worked for less. They wanted to be sure no woman would have a man's job when war ended. But they were not keen, either, that women should get the same wage as men for the same job.

Suffragettes

Before the war, women were not allowed to vote in elections for Parliament. Some women felt this was wrong and tried to persuade the govenment to change it. They were called *suffragettes*. Some of them became angry when the government would not listen. Led by Mrs Pankhurst, they began a campaign of violence. They were prepared to go to prison in order to make people take notice.

When war started their attitude changed. They did everything they could to help the war effort.

```
WOMEN'S SOCIAL AND POLITICAL
          UNION

       MRS PANKHURST
          Will speak at
        A PUBLIC MEETING
             At the
     ST. ANDREW'S HALL, GLASGOW.
    ON Tuesday March 16, at 8 pm.
            SUBJECT
        "WAR AND WAGES
  WHAT IS OUR DUTY TO THE NATION?"
```

1. Write out the name of Mrs Pankhurst's organisation, the WSPU.
2. Why would suffragettes not attack the government in war time?

Nurses

One way in which women could obviously help was nursing. Thousands became nurses and ambulance drivers. The nurses who joined the British Red Cross Society's Voluntary Aid Detachment were called VADs.

In an interview on an Imperial War Museum tape, one VAD describes her feelings after her first day's work in the Dundee Infirmary where wounded troops were cared for.

A group of nurses in France wrapped up against the cold

All night I could see those navy blue legs [*gangrene cases*] . . . but after I went in on Wednesday I was all right again, but I had to grit my teeth hard to keep myself [going], especially when I got that hand with no fingers on it. You see, the thing is that you feel you are helping.

Agnes Allan

1. What were VADs?

The Armed Forces

There were no women in the army until 1917 when the Women's Army Auxiliary Corps (WAAC) was organised. Members of the WAAC were to take over jobs which would release men to fight. Some worked as cooks or in offices. Others went to France where they might drive ambulances or work as gardeners in the huge cemeteries.

Women joined the Navy and Air Force too.

1. List the jobs done by women in the WAAC.
2. Why were there so many large cemeteries in France?
3. What job are the women in the photograph below doing?

The war gave women a chance to show that they were just as capable as men. The Prime Minister, Lloyd George, said,

It would have been utterly impossible for us to have waged a successful war had it not been for the skill, enthusiasm and effort which the women of this country have thrown into the war.

In 1918 women over 30 were allowed to vote.

6. Brave Men and Women

Edith Cavell

The story of Edith Cavell filled the main page of every newspaper in October 1915. Everyone in Britain was horrified. She was in charge of a training school for nurses in Belgium, and had been shot by the Germans as a spy. She had helped British soldiers to escape.

1. Why do you think people were so shocked by Edith Cavell's death?
2. What reasons would a German have given for her death?
3. How are spies usually treated in wartime?

Remembered by King and Country

The news of Bill Brown's death shocked his family. It was hard to believe they would never see him again. They received a scroll and, at the end of the war, three medals with Bill's name on them.

1. Suggest why a special medal was given to those who served in 1914–1915.
2. What might the Browns do with the scroll and the medals?

Some soldiers were decorated for bravery in action. 633 people received the highest award, the Victoria Cross. Other important awards were the Distinguished Service Order, the Distinguished Conduct Medal, the Military Cross and the Military Medal.

Brave Airmen

> *Victoria Cross*
> Extract from *London Gazette* of 8th June 1917; Captain Albert Ball, DSO, MC, late Notts and Derbyshire Regiment and RFC.
>
> 'For most conspicuous and consistent bravery from the 25th of April to the 6th of May 1917, during which period Captain Ball took part in twenty-six combats in the air and destroyed eleven hostile aeroplanes, drove down two out of control, and forced several others to land. In these combats Captain Ball, flying alone, on one occasion fought six hostile machines, twice he fought five, and once four. When leading two other British aeroplanes he attacked an enemy formation of eight. On each of these occasions he brought down at least one enemy. Several times his aeroplane was badly damaged, once so seriously that but for the most delicate handling his machine would have collapsed, as nearly all the control wires had been shot away. On returning with a damaged machine he had always to be restrained from immediately going out on another.
>
> In all, Captain Ball has destroyed forty-three German aeroplanes and one balloon, and has always displayed most exceptional courage, determination and skill.'

Members of Royal Flying Corps [RFC] often transferred from other regiments.
1. Why was this necessary at the start of the War?
2. Why was Captain Ball awarded the VC?

Edith Cavell

One of a series of admiring war postcards called 'Our Heroes'

In a letter home Captain Ball described how, after a long battle with a German flyer, both pilots ran out of ammunition.

There was nothing more to do after that, so we both burst out laughing . . . we flew side by side . . . and then we waved to each other and went off.

Captain Ball was shot down by German anti-aircraft guns on 8 May 1917 after he had shot down two German planes. The Germans buried him with great honour. A German pilot crossed the lines to drop a container with a note in it reporting the British pilot's death.

John Travers Cornwell, VC – this picture was painted after his death.

1. Suggest why the Germans buried Captain Ball with honour.
2. Why was it brave of the German to take the message reporting the British pilot's death?

Many nations had their own ace pilots. The French showered medals on Georges Guynemer; the Germans idolised the Red Knight, Baron Manfred Von Richthofen, who destroyed 80 Allied aircraft before being shot down in 1918.

A Brave Sailor

In the navy, too, many medals were awarded for gallantry. Everyone was moved by the story of Boy 1st Class John Travers Cornwell who died, aged 16, at the Battle of Jutland aboard HMS *Chester*. Altogether 6000 British sailors were killed at Jutland. John Cornwell won the VC for remaining at his post by one of the ship's guns after the rest of the gun crew had been killed or badly wounded. He died later of wounds.

A Brave Soldier

Look at the newspaper article on page 31.
1. How long had Piper Laidlaw been in the army?
2. Where did he win his VC?
3. Why would the piper and the Lieutenant in charge be first over the parapet of the trenches?
4. How did Piper Laidlaw help the charge?

HOW PIPER LAIDLAW WON THE V.C.

Piper Daniel Laidlaw, of the Scottish Borderers, who has been awarded the Victoria Cross is at present in Warwick Military Hospital.

He has eighteen years' service to his credit. He won his cross at Loos on September 25. 'On the Saturday morning,' he said, 'we got the order to take the German trenches. At 6.30 the bugler sounded the advance and I got over the parapet with Lieut. Young, who, I am sorry to say, has since been killed. I had the pipes going and the lads gave a cheer as they started towards the enemy's line.

'As soon as they showed over the trench top they began to fall very fast, but they never wavered, but dashed straight on, as I played the old air they all knew, "Blue Bonnets over the Border".

'I ran forward with them piping for all I knew, and just as we were getting near the German lines shrapnel caught me in the left ankle and leg. I was too excited to feel the pain just then.

'I kept on piping and piping, hobbling along after the laddies until I could go no more, and then, seeing that the boys had won the position, I began to get back as best I could to our own trenches. There does not seem much to tell, and I never thought that I should have won the grand decoration.'

Daily Record, 9 January 1916

First Tommy. "THE C.O.'S RECOMMENDED YOU FOR A V.C."
Second Tommy (half asleep and thinking of C.B.). "OH, LUMME! WHAT 'AVE I DONE NOW?"

After the war ended, soldiers hoped to find good jobs when they came home. This was not easy. Many found it difficult to get work. Joe Brown was lucky when he came back for he had a job waiting for him. But he found it hard to settle down and in 1921 he emigrated to Canada.

7. The War of Words

French Doctors Infect German Well with Plague Germs!

GERMANS CRUCIFY CANADIAN OFFICER!

GERMAN PRISONERS BLINDED BY ALLIED CAPTORS!

Belgian Child's Hands Cut Off by Germans!

These newspaper headlines printed during the First World War have one thing in common. They are all *untrue*.

1. Suggest which headlines are from (i) British, (ii) German newspapers. Say why.
2. How would people feel who read these stories?
3. Why might people believe such stories in wartime?
4. Newspapers did not check the facts as carefully as in peacetime. Suggest a reason.

The USA did not join the war until 1917 for Americans felt it was a European quarrel. Both Britain and Germany tried hard to win over the Americans to support them.

1. Why would Britain and Germany want American help?
2. How might they win support?

One Battle, Three Stories

> **ENEMY COMPELLED TO CEASE FIGHTING**
>
> **600 GERMANS SLAIN AT ONE POINT.**
>
> 28th April, 1915
>
> 1 – Fighting north and north-east of Ypres continued all yesterday.
> 2 – Our operations, in conjunction with the French, definitely stopped the German attack, and it has not since been renewed.
> 3 – Since yesterday morning there have been no Germans west of the Canal except at Steenstraate, where they have established a small bridge head.
> 4 – In resisting our counter-attacks the Germans have again made use of chlorine gas.

Here are accounts of the same battle which appeared in French and German newspapers.

> *Paris – First Report*
>
> To the north of Ypres our progress has been continued, especially on our left.
>
> We have taken six quick-firers, two bomb-throwers, and much material; and made several hundred prisoners, including several officers.
>
> The losses of the enemy were extremely high. At a single point on the front, in the proximity of the canal we counted more than six hundred German dead.
>
> On the heights of the Meuse, on the front Les Eparges-St Remy-Calonne trench, we have continued to gain ground, about one kilometre, and have inflicted on the enemy very severe losses.

Daily Record and Mail, 29 April 1915

BRITISH OFFENSIVE CHECKED

GERMAN OFFICIAL

In Flanders the British yesterday again attempted to regain the ground they had lost. In the afternoon they attacked from both sides of the road from Ypres to Pilken but the attack completely broke down 200 metres before our front. An evening attack further east failed, with severe British losses.

There was no attack on the west side of the canal.

In Champagne, we last night stormed an extensively fortified group, in spite of several counter-attacks. The enemy suffered heavy losses. We captured 60 unwounded Frenchmen, four machine guns and 13 trench mortars and howitzers.

The only strong French night attack in the Bois le Pretre was repulsed with great French losses.

Near Altkirch one of our airmen brought down a French aeroplane.

Daily Record and Mail, 29 April 1915

1. What impression would the Browns have of the battle?
2. What would a French reader believe had happened?
3. In what ways is the German account different?
4. Why are these stories different?
5. Each version mentions good points and omits bad news. Give examples of this.

Censorship

Newspapers had to rely on official information about the fighting. At first war correspondents were not allowed to write reports and later they were kept at base headquarters.

The Defence of the Realm Act listed certain things which must not be written about.

The number of troops and where they were.
Plans of future actions.
Movement of ships.
Information about munitions.

Even letters sent home by troops were opened and read by the Censor.

1. Why would the government not wish a full account to be published of what was happening at the front?
2. How might such information help the enemy?
3. Why was mail censored?
4. In wartime, governments concealed bad news and sometimes told lies in order to keep up the spirits of people at home. Do you think this was right? Say why.

MESSAGE FROM THE TRENCHES

What British Troops Want
CONFIDENT OF VICTORY

A deputation recently visited the Western Front.

The deputation brings a message from the trenches. Any idea of a strike in any branch of labour is, from the point of view of the soldiers, unthinkable.

"They say that with the co-operation of their brothers at home, they are confident of smashing the brutal Hun, and speedily ending the war.

"The cry is 'We want more men and more machine guns'."

Daily Record, November 1915

Advertisements and newspaper articles helped the war effort too

Wartime Songs

Everyone knew marching songs like, 'Pack up your troubles in your old kit bag' and 'It's a long way to Tipperary'. In the Music Halls they sang the soldiers' favourites, 'If you were the only girl in the world' and 'Goodbyee, don't cryee'.

But the soldiers at the front had other songs too. They joked about themselves as soldiers.

"HEARD THE LATEST RUMOUR UP FROM THE BACK, GEORGE? WAR'S GOING TO BE OVER NEXT WEEK."
"HO. WELL, I HOPE IT DON'T UPSET MY GOING ON LEAVE NEXT TUESDAY."

To the tune of a hymn they sang

> We are Fred Karno's* army
> A scruffy lot we are
> We cannot march. We cannot fight
> What blooming good are we?
> And when we get to Berlin
> The Kaiser he will shout
> 'Mein Gott, Mein Gott, what a ruddy fine lot
> Are the British Infantry.'

The only way to bear the horror of the trenches was to joke about it.

> I don't want to die, I don't want to die
> I don't want to go to the trenches again
> The Allemain [*German*] snipers they drive me insane
> I want to be – where those Jerries they can't snipe at me.
>
> Oh my – I don't want to die
> I want to go home.
>
> If you want to find your sweetheart
> I know where he is
> I know where he is, I know where he is
> If you want to find your sweetheart
> I know where he is
> Hanging on the front line wire.

When they sang

> There's a long, long, trail a'winding
> Into the land of my dreams

it must have seemed that home was very far

* *Fred Karno was a music-hall comedian.*

away and that the war would never end.

1. Why might soldiers feel people at home did not understand what war was like?
2. Why did soldiers sing songs which laughed at the horrors of war?
3. What were snipers? (See chapter 3.)
4. What was 'the front line wire'?

War Poems

Poets wrote of life in the trenches in a more serious way. They wanted to tell people what war was really like.

Siegfried Sassoon described a suicide in the trenches.

> I knew a simple soldier boy
> Who grinned at life in empty joy
> Slept soundly through the lonesome dark
> And whistled early with the lark.
>
> In winter trenches, cowed and glum
> With crumps [*noise made by a certain kind of shell*] and lice and lack of rum
> He put a bullet through his brain
> No one spoke of him again.
>
> You smug-faced crowds with kindling eye
> Who cheer when soldier lads march by
> Sneak home and pray you'll never know
> The hell where youth and laughter go.

Wilfred Owen, who was killed on the Western Front, described a gas attack

> Gas! Gas! Quick, boys! – an ecstasy of fumbling
> Fitting the clumsy helmets just in time.
> But someone still was yelling out and stumbling
> And flound'ring like a man in fire or lime.
> Dim through the misty panes and thick green light
> As under a green sea, I saw him drowning
> In all my dreams before my helpless sight
> He plunges at me, guttering, choking, drowning.

1. Why did the soldier shoot himself?
2. How did Sassoon feel about people at home who cheered soldiers on to fight?
3. How did the soldier in Owen's poem die?
4. How were the other soldiers saved from gas poisoning?
5. Why would he see 'through misty panes and thick green light'?
6. Why did Owen keep remembering the attack?

Anton Schnack, a German poet, described the same horror

> Death slaughters them, and they lie under weeds.
> Heavy, fossil, with hands full of spiders,
> Mouths scabbed red and brown.

Perhaps he and other German soldiers would have understood better than people at home why British soldiers sang 'Oh! Oh! Oh! what a lovely War!'

1.

2.

8. Looking at the Evidence

In order to find out what life was like during the First World War, we have looked at evidence or clues from that time. Just as a detective examines clues to build up a picture of what happened when a crime has been committed, a historian examines evidence to find out what happened in the past. Every piece of evidence adds to the picture.

Much of our evidence comes from photographs.

1. What do the photographs on this page and the next tell us about how messages were sent on the Western Front?
2. One of these photographs is German. The others are British. How can we tell that pictures 1 and 4 are British?
3. Which picture do you think shows German soldiers? Say why.

In an interview Mr James McCormack told how he was sent forward with two other signallers to the front line to set up a signalling base.

We were carrying flags, discs and a D111 telephone. We had a great struggle walking single file with all this equipment in the dark. The telephone was very heavy. We were tempted to dump it because we knew it wouldn't be much use anyway. The wires were easily smashed.

1. What other ways of sending messages are mentioned by Mr McCormack?
2. Use the information from these different sources to write a paragraph on sending messages in war time.

Although a long time has passed since the First World War began, there are still some old people who remember what life was like then.

1. If you had the chance to interview an old person about the war, what questions would you ask someone:
(a) who had been wounded at the battle of the Somme;
(b) who was only seven when the war began;
(c) who worked in a munitions factory during the war;
(d) who remembered his father telling how he won the Military Cross?

9. It Stopped at 11 o'clock

At eleven o'clock on the eleventh day of the eleventh month, 1918, the Great War ended. It had lasted four years, fourteen weeks and two days. Although the crowds cheered and sang, there were many who would never forget the terrible cost of the war. Over eight and a half million soldiers, mostly young men, had died. Another twenty million had been wounded. The lives of millions of people had been changed.

The war cost a lot in money too. All the money spent on weapons and explosives had been 'blown up'. Valuable ships and aeroplanes had been destroyed. The price of many goods had more than doubled. Most countries which had fought throughout the war were in debt. To pay back the money borrowed to pay for the war, governments asked people to pay high taxes. Those countries which had not done much fighting had been able to sell their goods to other countries. When the war ended Britain found it harder to sell her goods abroad. Many factories had to close down and men were out of work.

In France especially, farms, factories, roads and railways were in ruins

1. Why were there so many widows and unmarried women in the years after 1918?
2. Why did many countries have to borrow money during the War?
3. Suggest a reason why prices went up in wartime.
4. Why were taxes much higher after the War?
5. Why were men out of work when the War was over?
6. Why were so many areas destroyed in France?
7. Describe the feelings of the people in the picture as they look at the ruins of their farm.

Many countries changed their government. The rulers of Germany, Austria-Hungary and

Turkey gave up their thrones. The map of Europe looked very different.

1. *Why would these rulers no longer govern their countries?*
2. *Which other country had changed its ruler in 1917?*

Some good things came out of the War.

In the trenches rich and poor had fought and died side by side. People had begun to understand each other a little better. Working men felt they had fought for a better way of life.

Women had played an important part in the war effort. In peace time they were determined to keep the rights they had won.

Money had been spent during the War to improve wireless, aeroplanes, cars and buses. These improvements made a great difference to people's lives in peace time.

1. *Explain why people of different backgrounds came to understand each other better in wartime.*
2. *How had the war affected women's (i) work; (ii) pay; (iii) clothes?*
3. *What change took place in women's right to vote in 1918? (See chapter 5.)*
4. *How might wartime inventions and developments be useful in peacetime?*

One thing was certain; after the Great War things would never be quite the same again for anyone.

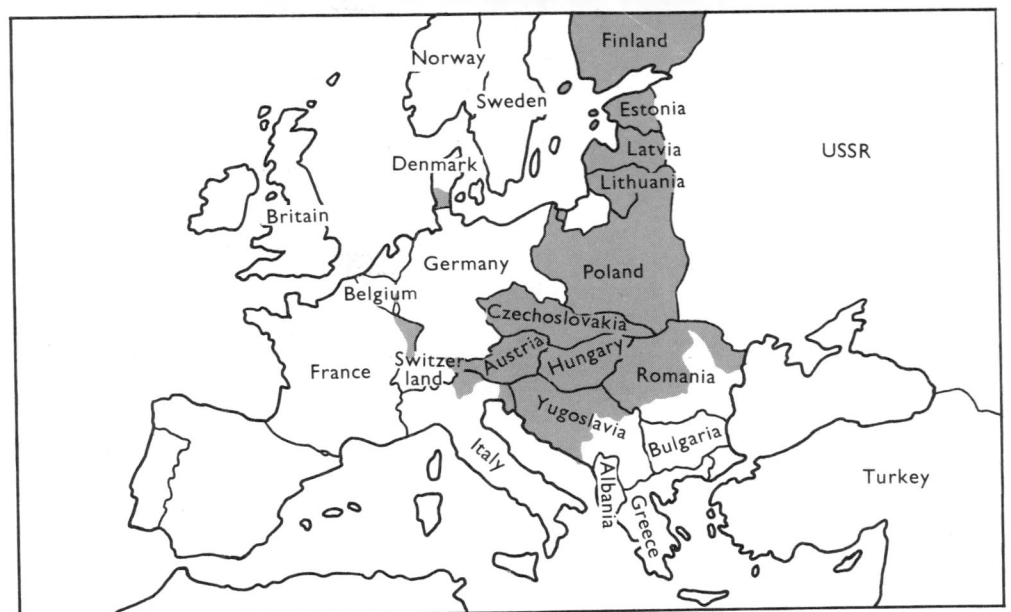

Europe in 1918 after the Great War. (The shaded area shows land losses by Austria-Hungary, Germany and Russia.)

Index

Air Aces 29, 30
Air Attacks 10, 11, 29
Air Service, Royal Naval 11
Airships 10
Allies 13, 14, 15

Balaclava 21
Barbed Wire 16
Bombardment 16
Budget (Brown family) 4

Casualties 22, 38
Cavalry 6
Cavell, Edith 29
Censorship 32, 33
Central Powers 14
Comforts 21
Communications, trenches 15; signallers 36, 37
Conscription 9
Court Martial 19
Cowardice 19
Czar 13

Death Sentences 19
Division 17
Dug-out 17

Eastern Front 14, 15
Family (Brown) 3
Feather, white 8
Food Shortages 13, 23

Gas 18, 32, 35
Guns 19, 33

Health 17
Horses 6
House (Browns') 4

Imperial Service 6

Jutland 12, 30

Kitchener 5

Leave 22
Lenin 13
Lice 18, 35
Loos 31

Machine Guns 19
Marne 14
Medals 29
Military Service Act 9
Mons 14
Munitions 23, 25, 26, 33

Navy, German 12; Royal 12
Nurses 27, 29

Pankhurst, Mrs E 27
Peace 38
Poems, War 35
Posters, Airship 10; Munitions 25; Recruiting 6, 7, 8
Prices 4, 38

Rationing 23
Rats 18
Recruiting, Benefits 7; Posters 6; Sergeant 5
Royal Flying Corps 29
Royal Naval Air Service 11
Russia 10, 13, 39

Sapping 16
Schmidts 24
Shortages 13, 23, 24
Shrapnel 19
Signallers 36
Sniping 16, 17
Somme 15, 17, 19
Songs 34, 35
Strikes 23, 24, 33
Submarines 13, 23
Suffragettes 27

Trade Unions 23
Trenches 15, 16, 17, 18 19, 20, 33, 35, 39

Uniform 9, 13, 17
USA 13, 15

V.A.D. 27
V.C. 29, 30, 31
Verdun 15
Volunteers 5

Ypres 14, 32, 33

Zeppelins 10, 11